SPORTS GOATs:
THE GREATEST OF ALL TIME

GOATs OF BASKETBALL

BY BRIAN MAHONEY

SportsZone

An Imprint of Abdo Publishing
abdobooks.com

abdobooks.com

Published by Abdo Publishing, a division of ABDO, PO Box 398166, Minneapolis, Minnesota 55439. Copyright © 2022 by Abdo Consulting Group, Inc. International copyrights reserved in all countries. No part of this book may be reproduced in any form without written permission from the publisher. SportsZone™ is a trademark and logo of Abdo Publishing.

Printed in the United States of America, North Mankato, Minnesota.
102021
012022

THIS BOOK CONTAINS
RECYCLED MATERIALS

Cover Photo: Ross D. Franklin/AP Images
Interior Photos: Bettmann/Getty Images, 4, 4–5; Bill Chaplis/AP Images, 6 (top), 6 (bottom); Paul Vathis/AP Images, 8, 9; Focus on Sport/Getty Images, 10, 10–11, 18 (top), 18 (bottom); Tony Tomsic/AP Images, 12–13, 13; Reed Saxon/AP Images, 14–15, 15; Jim Zerschling/Photo Researchers History/Archive Photos/Getty Images, 16, 17; Rick Stewart/ Getty Images Sport/Getty Images, 20, 20–21; Tom DiPace/AP Images, 22, 22–23; Michael Caulfield/AP Images, 24–25, 25; Branimir Kvartuc/AP Images, 26 (top), 26 (bottom); Rich Pedroncelli/AP Images, 28–29, 29; Ronald Martinez/AP Images, 30–31, 31; Ralph Freso/AP Images, 32–33, 33; AJ Mast/AP Images, 34–35, 35; Elaine Thompson/AP Images, 36, 36–37; Sue Ogrocki/AP Images, 38–39, 39; Eric Gay/AP Images, 40–41, 41; M. Anthony Nesmith/ Icon Sportswire/Getty Images, 42–43, 43

Editor: Charlie Beattie
Series Designer: Jake Nordby

Library of Congress Control Number: 2021941620

Publisher's Cataloging-in-Publication Data

Names: Mahoney, Brian, author.
Title: GOATs of basketball / by Brian Mahoney
Description: Minneapolis, Minnesota : Abdo Publishing, 2022 | Series: Sports GOATs: The greatest of all time | Includes online resources and index.
Identifiers: ISBN 9781532196492 (lib. bdg.) | ISBN 9781644947098 (pbk.) | ISBN 9781098218300 (ebook)
Subjects: LCSH: Basketball--Juvenile literature. | Basketball teams--Juvenile literature. | Basketball--Records--United States--Juvenile literature. | Professional athletes-- Juvenile literature.
Classification: DDC 796.323--dc23

TABLE OF CONTENTS

GEORGE MIKAN

The Lakers franchise has featured some of basketball's best big men. Wilt Chamberlain, Kareem Abdul-Jabbar, and Shaquille O'Neal all suited up for the team. But George Mikan started that tradition in the early 1950s. Mikan was the first superstar player in the National Basketball Association (NBA). He won five championships in six years from 1949 to 1954 with the Lakers. At that time, they played in Minneapolis. The Lakers moved to Los Angeles in 1960.

Mikan did not make the basketball team in his first year in high school. His coach cut him because he wore glasses. The coach didn't think Mikan could be a basketball player if he wore them.

But Mikan kept working on his skills and landed a scholarship to DePaul University in Chicago. He also grew to be 6 feet, 10 inches tall. Mikan swatted away so many balls going into the net that the National Collegiate Athletic Association (NCAA) established a goaltending rule to slow him down. That didn't stop Mikan, who led DePaul to the National Invitation Tournament (NIT) championship the next season.

Mikan began his professional career with a team called the Chicago American Gears in the National Basketball League (NBL). After that league folded, he went to the Lakers in a lottery. By 1954 he had led the league in scoring three times and rebounding twice. He was All-NBA six times before retiring at the age of 31.

Mikan was named the greatest player of the first half of the twentieth century by the Associated Press. The poll results were announced in 1950, while he was still an active player.

George Mikan averaged 22.3 points and 13.4 rebounds during his six seasons in the NBA.

BILL RUSSELL

Many debate who might be the NBA's greatest player ever. There's no question who the NBA's greatest champion is, though. Bill Russell easily holds that title.

The Boston Celtics won 11 titles in Russell's 13 seasons. That included eight in a row from 1959 to 1966. When Russell won his last

Bill Russell, *left*, celebrates his 10,000th NBA point with Boston Celtics head coach Red Auerbach in 1964.

two in 1968 and 1969, he both played and coached the team. In doing so, he became the first Black head coach in NBA history.

Most superstars are best known for their scoring. That wasn't the case for Russell. The center focused more on his defense and rebounding. He knew the Celtics had plenty of other players who could provide points.

That leadership helped him win two championships in college at the University of San Francisco. He also captained the United States to victory at the Olympics in 1956. However, he is best known for his play with the Celtics.

Russell is second in NBA history in rebounds, but no one grabbed more in the playoffs. Russell's 1,718 rebounds in NBA Finals games are almost twice as many as second place. He had two 40-rebound games in the NBA Finals.

Other players put up flashier numbers. But Russell's teams won more, and his all-around play was viewed as the biggest reason. Players voted him Most Valuable Player (MVP) of the league five times. Russell was never named MVP of the NBA Finals because the league did not give out the award until 1969, his last season. But when the league renamed the Finals MVP Award in 2005, it was named after Russell.

FAST FACT

During the 1961–62 season, Wilt Chamberlain averaged 50.4 points. Oscar Robertson averaged a triple-double for the season. But neither of those players was the NBA MVP. Bill Russell won his second of three in a row, as his 23.6 rebounds helped the Celtics to a 60-20 record.

WILT CHAMBERLAIN

On March 2, 1962, Wilt Chamberlain did something unthinkable. The 7-foot-1-inch Philadelphia Warriors center scored 100 points in a single game. It was an unforgettable moment in a career that saw the player known as the Big Dipper shatter NBA records.

A single NBA player has topped 70 points in a game only 11 times. Wilt Chamberlain had six of them. He scored 50 or more points 118 times. Michael Jordan is second on that list, with 31.

Some of his marks seem unbeatable. NBA games are 48 minutes long. During the 1961–62 season, Chamberlain averaged 48.5 minutes per game after overtimes were factored in.

His 23,924 rebounds are still the most in NBA history. And he retired as the NBA's leading all-time scorer. But he was also an excellent passer. During the 1967–68 season, Chamberlain led the NBA in assists.

Chamberlain was named Rookie of the Year in 1959–60. It was the start of a 14-year career with four different teams. He was an All-Star 13 times. The only season he missed out was 1969–70. That year he played only 12 regular-season games due to a knee injury.

FAST FACT

Hershey, Pennsylvania, is famous for more than chocolate. Some basketball superstars played there too. Wilt Chamberlain's 100-point game was played in Hershey, not Philadelphia. In 1996 Kobe Bryant won a Pennsylvania high school state championship there.

The only thing Chamberlain missed early in his career was an NBA championship. He finally won a title in 1967 with the Philadelphia 76ers. He won again in 1972 with the Los Angeles Lakers.

Chamberlain retired after the 1972–73 season, but not before setting one final record. At age 36, he made 72.3 percent of his field goals.

Wilt Chamberlain poses after scoring 100 points for the Philadelphia Warriors against the New York Knicks on March 2, 1962. The Warriors won the game, 169–147.

OSCAR ROBERTSON

O scar Robertson entered the NBA in the 1960–61 season with a unique blend of skills. Many NBA players are good scorers. Some are strong rebounders, and others are graceful passers. Robertson was a master at combining all three in the same game.

Robertson had 181 triple-doubles in his career. That was the most in NBA history until Russell Westbrook caught him in 2020–21. Robertson was the first player to average a triple-double for an entire season. In 1961–62 he averaged 30.8 points, 12.5 rebounds, and 11.4 assists per game. Nobody else did that until Westbrook in 2016–17.

Robertson was one of the first players to prove that point guards were more than just passers. They also could be great scorers. After setting 14 NCAA records in college at the University of Cincinnati, he averaged 30.5 points in his first NBA season of 1960–61. He was voted the Rookie of the Year.

But Robertson was at his best when setting up teammates. Robertson led the NBA in assists per game six times. For his career, he averaged 9.5 assists. Only Magic Johnson and John Stockton's career averages were higher.

Despite Robertson's excellent play, it looked for a while like he might never win a championship. It wasn't until 1971, in his eleventh season, that he finally won a title with the Milwaukee Bucks.

Robertson played three more years. When he finally retired in 1974, he had been an All-Star in 12 of his 14 seasons.

Oscar Robertson (1) makes a move while playing for the Milwaukee Bucks. Robertson spent the last four years of his career in Milwaukee after 10 years with the Cincinnati Royals.

Jerry West averaged over 30 points per game in four of his 14 NBA seasons.

JERRY WEST

From the moment he entered the league in 1960, Jerry West had a knack for hitting big shots in key moments. That skill earned him the nickname Mr. Clutch.

West averaged 27 points for his career, one of the highest totals in NBA history. In the playoffs, West was even better. He set a record by averaging 46.3 points in one playoff series. When he retired, his 1,679 points scored in NBA Finals games was a record.

Despite West's efforts, his Los Angeles Lakers kept coming up short against the Boston Celtics' dynasty of the 1960s. West's teams made the NBA Finals nine times. But he won only one NBA championship, in 1971–72. West was even voted MVP of the 1969 NBA Finals despite losing the series. He is the only person to win that award while playing on the losing side.

West was an All-Star 14 times, every year of his career. After his retirement from the Lakers, he continued to work for the team. He started coaching the team in 1976 and became its general manager in 1982.

Even today every NBA fan recognizes West. That's because when the NBA redesigned its logo in 1969, a white silhouette of West was chosen.

FAST FACT

West was a savvy team executive. He signed Shaquille O'Neal and traded for Kobe Bryant before Bryant ever played a game. West's moves helped the Lakers to eventually win six NBA championships.

Kareem Abdul-Jabbar, *left*, of the Los Angeles Lakers puts up a sky hook against the Seattle SuperSonics during a 1989 game.

KAREEM ABDUL-JABBAR

Kareem Abdul-Jabbar entered the NBA in 1969, and he brought his signature shot with him. He launched his famous "sky hook" from high over his right shoulder. Because he was 7 feet, 2 inches tall, the shot was almost impossible for defenders to block. Abdul-Jabbar used it to become the leading scorer in NBA history with 38,387 points. He scored at least 1,000 in every season except his last, in 1988–89.

That was just one of his many records. When Abdul-Jabbar retired in 1989 after 20 seasons, he was No. 1 in nine major statistical categories. The 19-time All-Star remained in the top three in rebounds and blocked shots more than 30 years after his career ended.

Abdul-Jabbar came to the NBA after one of the greatest college careers ever. Then still known as Lew Alcindor, he led the University of California, Los Angeles (UCLA) to the national championship three straight seasons from 1967 to 1969.

He was an instant NBA superstar with the Milwaukee Bucks. After the 1969–70 season, he was named Rookie of the Year. The next season Alcindor won the first of six MVP Awards. He converted to Islam in 1971 and took the name Kareem Abdul-Jabbar.

After leading the Bucks to their first title, Abdul-Jabbar joined the Lakers in 1975. The team made the playoffs 18 times with Abdul-Jabbar at center. In 10 of those seasons, the Lakers made the NBA Finals. He won five more NBA titles with the Lakers. And on April 5, 1984, he became the leading scorer in NBA history. The historic basket came on a sky hook.

LARRY BIRD

Before the three-point contest at the 1988 All-Star weekend, Larry Bird walked into the locker room and asked the rest of the competitors, "Who's coming in second?" Bird was confident he would win. And he did.

Oddly, Bird said he rarely practiced three-pointers because teams didn't shoot them very often when he played. He never attempted more than 237 in any season.

The Boston Celtics star instead piled up points in other ways. Bird finished his career with 21,791 points, averaging 24.3 per game. And that was far from all he did. Bird was also an incredible passer and strong rebounder. He finished with 59 triple-doubles.

Bird led the Celtics to three NBA championships. He was voted the league MVP three consecutive seasons from 1984 to 1986. It was Bird and Magic Johnson, playing for the rival Los Angeles Lakers, who helped raise the popularity of the NBA in the early 1980s.

Unfortunately back problems forced Bird to retire in 1992 after only 13 seasons. He enjoyed one last highlight first, playing on the 1992 US Olympic "Dream Team" of NBA stars that won the gold medal.

FAST FACT

The Dream Team is considered basketball's best team ever. With Bird, Magic Johnson, and Michael Jordan on the roster, the team averaged an Olympic-record 117.3 points.

After his playing career, Bird achieved more success in his home state of Indiana. He coached the Indiana Pacers to the NBA Finals. He later served as their team president. He is the only person to be voted NBA MVP, Coach of the Year, and Executive of the Year.

Larry Bird was the first player in NBA history to hit at least 50 percent of his field goals, 40 percent of his three-pointers, and 90 percent of his free throws in the same season.

MAGIC JOHNSON

His real name is Earvin Johnson. Basketball fans of the 1980s knew him by his nickname: Magic.

The NBA had never seen a player like Johnson when he entered the league in 1979. He was a point guard who stood 6 feet, 9 inches tall,

Magic Johnson, *right*, drives for a layup against Larry Bird of the Boston Celtics during the 1985 NBA Finals.

making him tall enough to play power forward. He could grab rebounds and then start the Los Angeles Lakers' fast break himself. Johnson often ended it by throwing a great pass to a teammate for an easy basket.

In 1979 Johnson won the college national championship at Michigan State University. He won the NBA championship the next year. He was the first rookie to be named NBA Finals MVP.

He showed his unique skills in the deciding game against the Philadelphia 76ers. With teammate Kareem Abdul-Jabbar injured, Johnson played center. He finished with 42 points and 15 rebounds. That championship began an era of flashy, high-flying Lakers basketball known as Showtime. The always-smiling Johnson was the star.

Johnson played in the NBA Finals nine times in his 12 full seasons. He won five championships. Three times he was the MVP of the regular season and three times MVP of the NBA Finals.

Johnson had to retire in November 1991 after learning he was infected with human immunodeficiency virus (HIV). But he returned to play in the 1992 NBA All-Star Game, winning MVP. He then won a gold medal with the US Dream Team in the 1992 Olympics. After another brief comeback in 1996, Johnson retired for good.

FAST FACT

Larry Bird and Magic Johnson met four times to decide championships, once before they even joined the NBA. Johnson's Michigan State Spartans beat Bird's Indiana State University for the 1979 NCAA title. Bird's Celtics beat Johnson's Lakers in the 1984 NBA Finals. The Lakers beat the Celtics in 1985 and 1987.

CHERYL MILLER

Cheryl Miller was the biggest women's basketball star of the 1980s. Her legendary feats gained national attention while she was still in high school.

She once scored 105 points in a game while playing for Riverside Polytechnic High School in California. And she set the California state record for points in a career with 3,405. Miller was the first high school player to be named an All-American four straight years.

Miller then led the University of Southern California (USC) to the top. Her all-around athleticism was a huge key to the Trojans' success. They won the first of two consecutive national titles in 1983, Miller's freshman year. In each of the next three years, she was voted Naismith Player of the Year.

USC has had other Hall of Fame players such as Lisa Leslie, Cynthia Cooper, and Tina Thompson. None of them could get close to some of the records that Miller set. She scored 3,018 points in college. She is also USC's career leader in rebounds and steals. Miller was voted an All-American all four years. She was also the leading scorer for the US Olympic team that won a gold medal in 1984.

After suffering a serious knee injury in 1987 at the age of 23, Miller's playing career ended. The Women's National Basketball Association (WNBA) did not exist at the time. Miller's accomplishments are often cited as a reason for its founding in the 1990s. She was voted into the James Naismith Memorial Basketball Hall of Fame in 1995.

Cheryl Miller rises for a jump shot while playing for USC in 1985.

MICHAEL JORDAN

Michael Jordan changed the basketball world the minute he took the floor for the Chicago Bulls in 1984. His scoring exploits, drive to win, and aggressive play style would make him famous beyond the sports arena.

The man nicknamed Air Jordan led the Bulls to six NBA titles in the 1990s, winning the NBA Finals MVP Award each time. It could have been even more, but Jordan retired from basketball in 1993 and missed most of the next two seasons while playing minor league baseball.

Jordan owns many NBA scoring records. His 30.1 points per game is the highest average in league history. He won a record 10 scoring titles, including seven in a row from 1986–87 to 1992–1993.

But he was at his best in the playoffs. Jordan averaged 33.4 points per game in the postseason. Against the mighty Boston Celtics in the 1986 playoffs, Jordan set a postseason record by scoring 63 points in a game. He scored a record 41.0 points per game in the 1993 championship series against the Phoenix Suns.

Jordan was a combination of talent and relentless intensity. Nothing mattered to him more than victory. And he won at every level. His last-second shot secured an NCAA title for the University of North Carolina in 1982. He also won Olympic gold medals in 1984 in Los Angeles and 1992 with the Dream Team in Barcelona, Spain.

His success brought fame like no NBA player before him. The trend of popular basketball sneakers began with his first Air Jordans in the 1980s. Jordan was basketball's first global celebrity, and his many endorsements made him one of the richest athletes on the planet.

Michael Jordan won five regular-season MVP Awards and was named All-NBA first team 10 times.

Shaquille O'Neal, *left*, powers his way to the basket while playing for the Los Angeles Lakers in 1996. O'Neal played eight years in Los Angeles and won three NBA titles.

SHAQUILLE O'NEAL

On April 23, 1993, rookie Shaquille O'Neal threw down a dunk so fiercely he collapsed the backboard. It almost landed on top of him. The moment was an early display of the muscle he would use to dominate opponents for nearly 20 years. And he would do it all with one of basketball's widest smiles.

O'Neal's 7-foot-1-inch, 325-pound frame made him nearly unstoppable. He powered his way to the top of the basketball world during his Hall of Fame career. He won four NBA titles, including three straight with the Los Angeles Lakers from 2000 to 2002. He was the MVP of the NBA Finals all three years.

O'Neal went on to win another title with the Miami Heat in 2006. He was in the postseason 17 times in his 19 seasons and ranked in the top five all-time in playoff points, rebounds, and blocked shots.

In addition to his thunderous dunks, O'Neal had a soft shooting touch. He led the NBA in field goal percentage 10 times, breaking Wilt Chamberlain's record. He twice led the league in scoring. And in both the 2000 and 2002 NBA Finals, he scored at least 30 points in every game.

O'Neal retired as one of the top 10 scorers in NBA history and one of the game's most beloved stars. He enjoyed giving playful nicknames to teammates, opponents, and himself. Following his retirement, he continued to use his fun personality to entertain fans during a successful television career as a sports analyst.

KOBE BRYANT

Kobe Bryant was 37 years old and had been an NBA player for 20 years when he played his last game in 2016. Instead of going out quietly, he scored 60 points.

Bryant's ability to score was legendary. Even late in his career, he still could have big nights at any time. His 81 points against the

Kobe Bryant averaged a career-high 35.4 points per game during the 2005–06 season.

Toronto Raptors in 2006 marked the closest anyone had come to Wilt Chamberlain's NBA-record 100-point night.

One of several players to jump straight from high school to the NBA in the 1990s, Bryant was barely 18 when he made his debut with the Los Angeles Lakers. After two seasons coming off the bench, he became a star. Bryant teamed up with Shaquille O'Neal to win three straight NBA championships from 2000 to 2002. Then he led the Lakers to two more in 2009 and 2010. He was the NBA Finals MVP both of those years.

Bryant wowed fans with his ability to make tough shots. His signature shot was a fadeaway jumper. Fired off while Bryant was falling away from the basket, the shot was tough to block. It was one of the reasons he was able to take, and make, so many game-winning shots in his career.

Bryant played his whole career with the Lakers. By the time he retired, only two players had scored more than Bryant's 33,643 points. Bryant also had a legendary competitive streak. Most players don't take the All-Star game seriously, but Bryant did. He was the game's MVP four times. The NBA later renamed the game's MVP Award after him.

Tragically, Bryant died in a helicopter crash in January 2020 when he was only 41. He was voted into the Hall of Fame three months later after the normal three-year waiting period was waived.

FAST FACT

Teams often retire the uniform numbers of great players. The Lakers retired two numbers for Kobe Bryant. He wore No. 8 for his first 10 seasons then switched to No. 24 for his final 10.

Lisa Leslie, *left*, rises for a layup during a 1997 game for the Los Angeles Sparks.

LISA LESLIE

Lisa Leslie made history in 2002 when she became the first player to dunk in a WNBA game. She was doing amazing things on the court long before that.

In 1982 Cheryl Miller had set a record by scoring 105 points in a high school game. In 1990 Leslie scored 101 points in a game, and she did it in only one half. By then she was already receiving hundreds of college scholarship offers. The 6-foot-5-inch Leslie chose USC, where she was a three-time All-American and the first player to be chosen to the All-Pac-10 Conference team four times.

Leslie was in the first group of players to join the WNBA for its opening season in 1997. By 2001 she was on top of the league. She was the first WNBA player to be named MVP of the regular season, All-Star Game, and WNBA Finals in the same year. Her Los Angeles Sparks won their first championship that season. They won again in 2002, and Leslie was once again the WNBA Finals MVP.

Leslie spent 12 seasons in the WNBA. During that time, she was one of the league's most recognizable players. She was the league's MVP three times and an All-Star eight times. When she retired, she was the league's career leader in scoring and rebounding.

Leslie was also the first basketball player to be an Olympic gold medalist four times, from 1996 to 2008. At the end of her career with the national team, she was the team's all-time leading scorer, rebounder, and shot blocker.

Tim Duncan, *right*, was named to the All-NBA first team 10 times in his career. He was also named to the second team seven times.

TIM DUNCAN

Growing up on the small island of St. Croix in the US Virgin Islands, Tim Duncan was a nationally ranked swimmer. Everything changed when he was 14 and a hurricane destroyed his local pool. Needing something to do, Duncan picked up a basketball for the first time. He soon went on to become one of the best players in the sport's history.

Even from the start, Duncan was a natural on the court. The tall but skinny teenager whom few in the United States had seen just needed a chance. Wake Forest University coach Dave Odom decided to give him one. In four years, Duncan went from raw talent to the two-time Atlantic Coast Conference (ACC) player of the year. Then the San Antonio Spurs selected him first overall in the 1997 NBA Draft.

In an era filled with brash, talkative players, Duncan stood out by saying very little. He let his game do the talking. Duncan had smooth footwork. He also developed the softest shooting touch of any big man in NBA history. He was especially known for his bank shot. At 6 feet, 11 inches, he could soar above opponents and tap the ball in off the backboard. Fellow great Shaquille O'Neal nicknamed Duncan the Big Fundamental for his old-school skills.

Duncan's interior dominance helped the Spurs win five championships in his 19-year career. He was named the MVP of the NBA Finals in three of those victories. By the time he retired after the 2015–16 season, Duncan had won two MVP Awards and was named All-NBA 15 times.

Through 2020 Sue Bird had been named to eight All-WNBA teams in her career.

SUE BIRD

When Sue Bird wore red, white, and blue, she was as good as gold. One of the best point guards ever, she led her teams to multiple championships in college, the WNBA, and overseas. But she may have made her biggest mark playing for her country. Bird won the most combined medals of any player in the Olympics and the World Cup.

Bird's legendary leadership skills paced the powerhouse program at the University of Connecticut (UConn) to national championships in 2000 and 2002. The 2002 team finished undefeated, and she was the National Player of the Year.

That summer Bird was the first pick in the WNBA draft by the Seattle Storm. Despite two knee surgeries, she was still going strong at age 40, winning her fourth championship in 2020. The Storm also won in 2004, 2010, and 2018. Through the 2021 season, Bird was the WNBA's all-time leader in assists and games started.

On top of her WNBA success, Bird also played overseas for three different Russian club teams from 2004–05 to 2012–13. In that time, her teams won five titles in EuroLeague, a cup competition that features the best teams in Europe, including four straight from 2007 to 2010.

Bird's international career began in 2002, just after she left Connecticut. By 2021 she had played in 10 major international tournaments. At the World Cup, she collected four gold medals and one bronze. In 2021 at the Olympics in Tokyo, Japan, Bird joined teammate Diana Taurasi as the first five-time Olympic gold medalists in basketball.

LeBron James of the Miami Heat throws down a dunk during the 2012 Eastern Conference finals against the Indiana Pacers. James won his first career NBA championship that season.

LEBRON JAMES

LeBron James drew comparisons to the NBA's legendary players when he was still in high school in Akron, Ohio. He was dubbed King James at age 17. Those who saw him play saw a 6-foot-9-inch kid with the passing ability of Magic Johnson and the scoring skills of Michael Jordan. Nearly two decades after being the first selection in the 2003 NBA Draft, those comparisons are still being made.

Prior to taking James with that first pick, the Cleveland Cavaliers had been to the playoffs only once in seven years. With James they made the postseason five straight seasons from 2005–06 to 2009–10, including the Finals once.

But James's Cavs kept coming up short of a title. In 2010 he famously left Cleveland for Miami. He captured two NBA titles with the Heat before returning to Cleveland for the 2014–15 season. The next year, he brought the city its first NBA title. During game 7 of that year's Finals against the Golden State Warriors, James delivered his most famous play. With 1:50 remaining of an 89–89 tie, James chased down Warriors forward Andre Idguodala and swatted away his breakaway dunk attempt. James's amazing effort was simply dubbed "the Block."

In 2018 he brought his combination of size and skill to the Western Conference with the Los Angeles Lakers. In 2020 he delivered yet another NBA title as the Lakers knocked off Miami in the Finals.

Repeatedly, James has earned all those comparisons to NBA greats that began back when he was in high school. In 2020 he tied Jordan's record by becoming only the second player to win the MVP in both the regular season and NBA Finals four times.

DIANA TAURASI

After UConn won the 2002 women's college championship, four of its players were taken in the first six picks of the WNBA Draft. Many wondered if a team that lost so much talent could stay on top. But the Huskies still had Diana Taurasi. She led UConn to another title in 2003 and then a third in 2004. The guard was the Most Outstanding Player of the Final Four in both years. Taurasi then set out on what may be the finest pro career ever.

As the WNBA entered its twenty-fifth season in 2021, Taurasi's name was all over its record book. She was No. 1 all-time in points and three-pointers, and she ranked fourth in assists. She led the league in scoring five times and assists once.

Taurasi plays with extreme confidence, always believing she can take her team to victory. Phoenix Mercury general manager Jim Pitman called the guard the "best winner and competitor in the women's game."

Taurasi has used that to help her teams win championships around the world. That includes three WNBA titles with the Mercury, six championships for teams in Europe, and gold medals in five Olympics and three World Cups.

Her long list of honors included the 2009 WNBA MVP Award. Through 2020 she had been named to the All-WNBA first team 10 times and the second team in four other seasons. In June of 2021, Taurasi became the first WNBA player to break the 9,000-point mark. No other player in the history of the league had even 7,500.

Diana Taurasi became the first player to score over 800 points in a WNBA season in 2006, when she put up 860.

Through the 2020–21 season, Kevin Durant was one of only six all-time NBA players with a career scoring average over 27 points per game.

KEVIN DURANT

The University of Texas is best known for its football teams. Practically overnight Kevin Durant made the Longhorns' basketball team a must-see show. The skinny, 6-foot-10 kid who could play like a guard or a forward averaged 25.8 points per game. At the end of the 2006–07 season, he was the first freshman ever to win the prestigious Wooden Award as national player of the year.

Durant didn't slow down once he reached the NBA. He started his career with the Seattle SuperSonics. They moved after his rookie season to become the Oklahoma City Thunder. No matter where he played, Durant was a problem for defenders. He was too quick for big men. With smaller players, he used his 7-foot, 2-inch wingspan to launch his accurate jump shot over them. The result was one of the most prolific scoring careers in NBA history. In his first seven seasons, Durant led the league in scoring four times. Twice he averaged over 30 points per game.

Before the 2016–17 season, Durant joined the Golden State Warriors. He instantly made the league's best team even better, leading them to the next two NBA titles—while winning MVP honors both times.

The Brooklyn Nets were Durant's next stop. They won 48 games in his first season, in 2020–21. That was up from 35 the previous year. Again he was stellar in the playoffs. Though the Nets lost a thrilling seven-game Eastern Conference semifinals to the Milwaukee Bucks, Durant delivered. His 48 points in the deciding game of the series were the most in a Game 7 in playoff history.

Stephen Curry averaged a career-best 5.3 three-point shots per game during the 2020–21 season, when he led the NBA in scoring at 32.0 points per game.

STEPHEN CURRY

The NBA added the three-point line for the 1979–80 season. That year only three teams made more than 100 three-point shots all season. In April 2021, Stephen Curry hit 96 in one month. Curry's long-range ability helped change the way the game was played in the NBA. Teams began to shoot more three-pointers after seeing his success with the Golden State Warriors.

Curry's shooting was so spectacular that fans began arriving early just to watch him warm up. He would practice shots that were far away from the basket. Some would come from near midcourt, and some would even come from out of bounds. Then in the games, Curry would do things that had never been done before. From November 2014 to February 2016, Curry hit at least one three-pointer in a record 157 consecutive games.

Curry led the NBA in three-pointers made for five straight seasons, from 2012–13 through 2016–17. He made more than 300 in two of those seasons, including an NBA-record 402 in 2015–16.

That dangerous outside shot helped the Warriors build a dynasty. Curry helped Golden State win NBA championships in 2015, 2017, and 2018. During their first championship run, he averaged 28.3 points and 6.4 assists while hitting 98 three-pointers in 21 playoff games. Golden State almost won four in a row. The Warriors set an NBA record with 73 wins in 2015–16 but lost to the Cleveland Cavaliers in the NBA Finals.

Curry was voted NBA MVP for 2014–15 and 2015–16. The second time, he was the first player to win the award in a unanimous vote.

Maya Moore averaged 18.4 points and 5.9 rebounds per game during her eight-year WNBA career.

MAYA MOORE

Maya Moore won a lot of games as a high school star in Georgia. Then she joined a dominant University of Connecticut program and won a lot more, including 90 games in a row. The winning didn't stop in the WNBA either. After the 2017 season, her seventh with the Minnesota Lynx, a journalist decided to add it all up. Moore's career record was 500-80. That's about as good as the historic 2015–16 Golden State Warriors, who went 73-9.

The Lynx had only two winning records in their first 12 WNBA seasons. After Moore joined in 2011, the Lynx became a dynasty. Moore led Minnesota to a 27–7 record and a league title that season. She was also named Rookie of the Year.

Over the next five seasons, the Lynx won three additional championships. Moore played a major role in their success. In 2013 she was MVP of the WNBA Finals. The next season she won the league scoring title and was named WNBA MVP. In Game 3 of the 2015 Finals against the Indiana Fever, Moore's buzzer beater turned the series around. The Lynx won in five games. She also added Olympic gold with Team USA in 2012 and 2016.

After the 2018 season, Moore turned her focus to a cause other than winning basketball games. She abruptly left the sport to fight for criminal justice reform in the United States. One of Moore's causes was overturning the wrongful conviction of a man named Jonathan Irons. Not only did Moore see Irons's sentence overturned, but she later married him.

HONORABLE MENTIONS

ELGIN BAYLOR

Baylor was voted to the All-NBA First Team 10 times as a forward with the Minneapolis and Los Angeles Lakers before retiring in 1972.

MOSES MALONE

The center jumped straight from high school to the American Basketball Association (ABA) in 1974. He joined the NBA two years later and went on to win MVP three times.

ISAIAH THOMAS

The point guard made 12 All-Star teams and guided the rugged Detroit Pistons to back-to-back NBA championships in 1989 and 1990.

CHARLES BARKLEY

The burly forward won the 1992–93 MVP Award and made 11 All-Star teams while averaging 11.7 rebounds per game during his 16-year career.

SHERYL SWOOPES

Swoopes won three WNBA MVP Awards while leading the Houston Comets to the league's first four titles from 1997 to 2000.

ALLEN IVERSON

Known for his devastating crossover dribble and ability to hit tough shots, the fearless guard won four scoring titles in his 14-year career and was named NBA MVP in 2000–01 after leading the Philadelphia 76ers to their first NBA Finals appearance in 18 years.

DIRK NOWITZKI

The German-born Nowitzki scored the most NBA points of any player born outside the United States. A power forward, he led the Dallas Mavericks to their first NBA championship in 2011.

TAMIKA CATCHINGS

In addition to retiring as the WNBA's all-time leading scorer in 2016, the forward was one of the league's best defensive players. She averaged 2.4 steals in her career.

GLOSSARY

assist
A pass that leads directly to a basket.

average
The number after a player's total of any statistic is divided by his or her games played.

draft
A system that allows teams to acquire new players coming into a league.

endorsement
When an athlete promotes a company in exchange for their products or money.

fast break
Moving the ball up the floor quickly.

field goal percentage
The number of shots a player made divided by the number he or she took.

goaltending
Blocking a shot after the ball has already finished rising.

rebound
To catch the ball after a shot has been missed.

rookie
A professional athlete in his or her first year of competition.

scholarship
Money awarded to a student to pay for education expenses.

steal
To take the ball from a player on the other team.

triple-double
Accumulating 10 or more of three certain statistics in a game.

MORE INFORMATION

BOOKS

Bryant, Howard. *Legends: The Best Players, Games, and Teams in Basketball*. New York: Puffin Books, 2017.

Flynn, Brendan. *The NBA Encyclopedia for Kids*. Minneapolis, MN: Abdo Publishing, 2022.

Howell, Bryan. *LeBron James vs. Michael Jordan*. Minneapolis, MN: Abdo Publishing, 2018.

ONLINE RESOURCES

To learn more about the GOATs of basketball, please visit **abdobooklinks.com** or scan this QR code. These links are routinely monitored and updated to provide the most current information available.

INDEX

ABOUT THE AUTHOR

Brian Mahoney has been a national NBA writer for the Associated Press since 2005, covering the NBA Finals, All-Star Games, and international basketball events such as the Olympics and World Cup. Based in New York, Mahoney covers the Knicks and Nets, along with providing coverage of boxing and tennis events. He is a 1995 graduate of the University of Connecticut, where he started his career covering the women's basketball team that won the